My Family

Blended Families

by Sarah L. Schuette

Consulting Editor: Gail Saunders-Smith, PhD

CAPSTONE PRESS
a capstone imprint

Pebble Books are published by Capstone Press,
151 Good Counsel Drive, P.O. Box 669, Mankato, Minnesota 56002.
www.capstonepress.com

Printed in the United States of America in North Mankato, Minnesota
092009
005618CGS10

Library of Congress Cataloging-in-Publication Data
Schuette, Sarah L., 1976–
    Blended families / by Sarah L. Schuette.
    p. cm. — (Pebble books. My family)
    Includes bibliographical references and index.
    Summary: "Simple text and photographs present blended families, including
how family members interact with one another" — Provided by publisher.
    ISBN 978-1-4296-3978-1 (library binding)
    ISBN 978-1-4296-4835-6 (paperback)
    1. Stepfamilies — Juvenile literature. I. Title. II. Series.
HQ759.92.S38 2010
306.874'7 — dc22   2009023382

Note to Parents and Teachers

The My Family set supports national social studies standards
related to identifying family members and their roles in the family.
This book describes and illustrates blended families. The images
support early readers in understanding the text. The repetition of
words and phrases helps early readers learn new words. This book
also introduces early readers to subject-specific vocabulary words,
which are defined in the Glossary section. Early readers may need
assistance to read some words and to use the Table of Contents,
Glossary, Read More, Internet Sites, and Index sections of the book.

Table of Contents

About Blended Families

Blended families are made of two or more families. They are also called stepfamilies.

A man becomes a stepfather
when he marries
a woman with children.

8

A woman becomes
a stepmother
when she marries
a man with children.

Jason

Jim

Kent

Siblings

Siblings are part
of blended families.
Jason and Jim are stepsiblings.
Jason's father is Kent.
Kent married Jim's mother.

Billy's dad and stepmother
had a daughter named Pam.
Pam and Billy
are half siblings.

Having Fun

Blended family members have fun together. Bobby and his stepmother bake cookies.

Mindy and her stepbrother pick out a family pet.

José and his half sister
go shopping.

Blended family members love each other.

Glossary

half sibling — a brother or sister who shares one birth parent with another child

member — a part of a group or family

sibling — a brother or a sister

stepfather — a man who marries a woman with children; the man becomes the children's stepfather.

stepmother — a woman who marries a man with children; the woman becomes the children's stepmother.

stepsibling — the son or daughter of a stepfather or stepmother

Read More

Hewitt, Sally. *My Stepfamily.* How Can I Deal With? Mankato, Minn.: Smart Apple Media, 2009.

Johnson, Julie. *Our Stepfamily.* Thoughts and Feelings. Mankato, Minn.: Stargazer Books, 2008.

Internet Sites

FactHound offers a safe, fun way to find Internet sites related to this book. All of the sites on FactHound have been researched by our staff.

Here's all you do:

Visit *www.facthound.com*

FactHound will fetch the best sites for you!

23

Index

Word Count: 106
Grade: 1
Early-Intervention Level: 10

Editorial Credits
Gillia Olson, editor; Juliette Peters, designer; Sarah Schuette, photo stylist; Marcy Morin, studio scheduler; Eric Manske, production specialist

Photo Credits
All photos by Capstone Studio/Karon Dubke

The author dedicates this book in memory of her grandmother, Janet Schuette Stender, who mothered a large blended family.